RL ___5.2___ Pts _1.0___

CONSTRUCTION WORKER

By Geoffrey M. Horn

Reading Consultant: Susan Nations, M.Ed.,
author/literacy coach/consultant in literacy development

Gareth Stevens
Publishing

Please visit our web site at **www.garethstevens.com.**
For a free catalog describing Gareth Stevens Publishing's list of high-quality books, call 1-800-542-2595 (USA) or 1-800-387-3178 (Canada). Gareth Stevens Publishing's fax: 1-877-542-2596

Library of Congress Cataloging-in-Publication Data
Horn, Geoffrey M.
    Construction worker / Geoffrey M. Horn.
        p. cm. — (Cool careers)
    Includes bibliographical references and index.
    ISBN-10: 0-8368-9192-9   ISBN-13: 978-0-8368-9192-8 (lib. bdg.)
    ISBN-10: 0-8368-9325-5   ISBN-13: 978-0-8368-9325-0 (softcover)
    1. Building—Vocational guidance—Juvenile literature.   2. Construction workers—Juvenile literature.   I. Title.
    TH159.H66   2009
    690.023—dc   2008012083

This edition first published in 2009 by
Gareth Stevens Publishing
A Weekly Reader® Company
1 Reader's Digest Rd.
Pleasantville, NY 10570-7000 USA

Senior Managing Editor: Lisa M. Herrington
Editor: Joann Jovinelly
Creative Director: Lisa Donovan
Designer: Paula Jo Smith
Photo Researcher: Kimberly Babbitt

Picture credits: Cover, title page: Alberto Incrocci/Getty Images; p. 4 AP Images; p. 5 AP Images/Ed Andrieski; p. 6 © Construction Photography/Corbis; p. 7 © Art on File/Corbis; p. 9 © Construction Photography/Corbis; p. 10 © Construction Photography/Corbis; p. 12 Liquidlibrary/Jupiter Images; p. 14 Image Source/Getty Images; p. 15 © SW Productions/ Brand X/Corbis; p. 16 © Jim Zuckerman/Corbis; p. 19 © Sorbo Robert/Corbis Sygma; p. 20 Karim Sahib/AFP/Getty Images; p. 21 Stone/Getty Images; p. 23 © Joel W. Rogers/Corbis; p. 24 © Lance Nelson/Corbis; p. 25 (top) © Somos Images/Corbis; pp. 26–27 Miric/Alamy; p. 27 AP Images/Ed Andrieski; p. 28 © Chuck Choi/Corbis

Printed in the United States of America

1 2 3 4 5 6 7 8 9 10 09 08

CONTENTS

Words in the glossary appear in **bold** type the first time they are used in the text.

CHAPTER 1

MANY TASKS, ONE TEAM

Super Bowl XLII will go down in sports history. The New York Giants beat the New England Patriots in a thrilling come-from-behind victory. The game was incredible — and so was the stadium where the two teams played. The University of Phoenix Stadium in Glendale, Arizona, opened in 2006. The stadium is home to the NFL's Arizona Cardinals. It took about 3,500 construction workers nearly three years to build.

One of the most amazing parts of the new stadium is its movable floor. The grass field is planted on a giant rolling tray. Most of the time, the tray sits outside

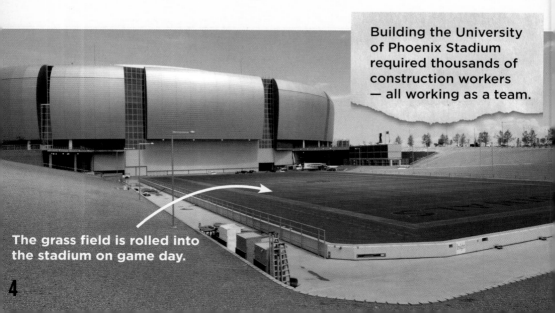

Building the University of Phoenix Stadium required thousands of construction workers — all working as a team.

The grass field is rolled into the stadium on game day.

the stadium in the warm Arizona sun. On game day, the grass-covered tray rolls back into the stadium. In just 75 minutes, a bare concrete floor changes into a beautiful, grassy indoor field.

Carpenters frame a new home near Denver, Colorado.

What Construction Workers Do

Construction workers build more than stadiums. They also build homes, schools, and hospitals. They dig tunnels and raise bridges. They lay floors and repair roofs. They use hand tools that can fit in a standard tool belt — and giant construction **cranes** that tower over big cities. They blast, scrape, cut, hammer, paint, and polish almost anything you can imagine.

Construction is a big business. Each year, worldwide spending on building projects totals more than $4 trillion. In the United States alone, yearly construction spending is more than $1 trillion. Millions of Americans work in construction. Many work for construction firms. Others are self-employed.

Do you enjoy hanging out at a brand-new shopping mall? Construction workers built it. Do you ride to school on paved roads? Construction workers built those, too.

Think of everything you do when you come home. Do you flick on the light switch? Flush the toilet? Turn on the TV? You can do all these things because of workers in the building trades. They put in the wires and pipes that keep your home running smoothly.

Builders — Old and New

People have been building things for a very long time. In ancient Egypt, thousands of builders worked on the great pyramids at Giza. In Europe, workers labored to

Workers pour concrete into a reinforced slab — a common method in modern construction.

build huge castles. Much of this work was done by hand, using basic tools and simple machines. Materials were also simple — stones, wood, or mud bricks.

Today construction in the United States and other modern countries is much more advanced. Projects are planned and managed by computer. Gigantic earth-moving machines clear the way for new buildings. Construction crews use **lasers** and other high-tech tools. Space-age designs make skyscrapers taller and stronger than ever before.

Space-age designs were used to build the Walt Disney Concert Hall in Los Angeles, California.

Working as a Team

More than ever, construction crews understand they must work as a team. Teamwork is the key to finishing a job on time and under budget. Even a small project needs many different skills. For example, building a house may involve bricklayers, carpenters, and roofers. It may also require electricians, plumbers, and other people with specific skills.

The construction crew must do the job right — and in the right order. For instance, wiring and pipes go inside walls. Electricians and plumbers must do their work before walls are finished and painted. If the wiring and pipes behind a finished wall need to be redone, the wall must be refinished, too. That costs both time and money.

Safety also depends on teamwork. Crews that deal with heavy machines and high **scaffolding** run big risks. They must work together carefully and use the proper safety equipment to ensure that no one gets hurt.

Is Construction the Right Career for You?

Did you like building with blocks and connecting toys when you were young? Do you still enjoy taking things apart and putting them back together? Do you take pride in working with your hands? Would you prefer to move around to different job sites rather than sit at a desk each day? Do you enjoy working as part of a team? If so, construction may be the right career for you.

On the Job: Construction Worker

Pamela Novotny lives in New Hampshire. She works on highways and bridges. She learned through an on-the-job training program. "I love being able to work outside and to really be able to use my hands and get them dirty," she says. "You really feel like you've accomplished something at the end of the day."

For some construction jobs, you'll have to feel comfortable working outdoors in high places.

There are many different ways to launch a career in construction. Some workers begin right after high school. Many high schools also offer classes that teach **vocational** skills such as electrical wiring. Other young people interested in careers in construction often start as helpers, learning skills from experienced workers. Some may take courses in private trade schools. Companies and **labor unions** may also provide on-the-job training. If you want to design or manage a project, you'll need a college degree.

Construction can be hard work. But the pay is good. Workers earn more than $20 an hour, on average. For skilled workers, long-term job prospects are excellent.

CHAPTER 2

WHO WORKS IN CONSTRUCTION?

Every construction project requires a variety of workers. A few people run each project. These are the managers. A second group prepares the construction site. These workers survey the land and make it suitable for building. A third group puts up the main structure and makes sure it's safe.

Roads, driveways, and parking lots need a smooth coat of asphalt before they are ready to use.

A great deal of construction work is done by **trade contractors.** These firms or workers have special skills. They include electricians, carpenters, painters, and plumbers.

Construction Managers

Construction managers plan and direct the project. They must be on call twenty-four hours a day. Construction workers may need to work nights, weekends, and holidays. Managers may need to work similar shifts.

Good managers are important to any project's success. They spot and correct safety problems. They help manage the budget. They keep the project on schedule. Most managers have a college degree.

On the Job: Construction Manager

Pat Pellegrino, Jr., lives in Pennsylvania. His father was a carpenter, and his grandfather was a bricklayer. After high school, Pellegrino trained as a carpenter. Later he became a manager for L.F. Driscoll, a construction firm based in Philadelphia, Pennsylvania.

Safety is a must for Pellegrino. "If you want to walk a beam, you have to be safe," he says. "You have to wear a harness and a hardhat, safety glasses, and gloves."

An excavator prepares a site for future construction.

Structural Engineers

Buildings and bridges must be tough. They must stand up to heavy loads, high winds, and earthquakes. Making sure that buildings are tough enough is a job for a structural engineer.

Structural engineers work with architects to develop new designs or improve existing ones. They also inspect structures while they are being built. This is to make sure the structures meet all requirements. Structural engineers must have at least a college degree in engineering.

Land Surveyors

Before construction begins, builders must first choose a site. Then they must decide how to prepare the site for the new building. These jobs are done by land surveyors. They measure the land. They look carefully at its shape and surface. Then they help decide where the building can best be placed. Land surveyors often have college degrees in civil engineering.

Equipment Operators

Building site work often requires big machines and the people to run them. Equipment operators control the heavy machines that move earth and building materials. These machines include bulldozers, cranes, **excavators**, and **pile drivers**.

Many equipment operators work at night. They must pay close attention to safety. They may also have to fix machines that break down.

Iron and Metal Workers

Iron and metal workers install the giant steel girders and columns that support large buildings and bridges. They also form the steel mesh that supports concrete highways and tunnels. Some of these people work on site. Others work in iron and steel mills that produce metal parts. Most workers learn skills on the job or as an **apprentice**.

A bricklayer shares his know-how with a young apprentice.

Starting Out

Apprentice programs are common in the construction trades. Beginners get on-the-job training alongside experienced workers. They also learn the trade through classroom study. An apprentice program may take several years. During that time, the apprentice may earn less than a fully skilled worker in the same field.

Electricians

Electricians install the wires, fuses, switches, and circuits that give a building its electric power. They use special equipment to test the wiring and ensure its safety. Many electricians work for themselves.

Electricians must pass a special test. Cities and towns have codes that spell out how electrical systems should be installed. Electricians must understand these codes and safety standards.

Cutting wires is part of an electrician's job.

Carpenters

Carpenters work with wood. Some build wooden forms that are later filled with concrete. Others build the frames for houses. Nearly one-third of the 1.5 million American carpenters are self-employed. Most learn the trade through on-the-job training.

Drywall Installers

Drywall is used for the **interior** walls of most buildings. It is sometimes called wallboard or Sheetrock. Drywall installers cut this material to fit atop the wooden or steel frames of a building. The installers must "finish"

Drywall is used for inside walls and ceilings.

Repair and Remodeling

Paint fades. Carpets wear thin. Heating systems break down. Many workers in the building trades spend much of their time repairing things that wear out.

Even when the materials are in good working order, the needs of people using the building may change. **Remodeling** jobs make major changes to meet those needs. In homes, kitchen or bathroom remodeling is very popular. Smaller projects like these are another source of construction work.

the wall so the seams between separate sheets of drywall cannot be seen. The drywall is then prepared for painting. Workers usually learn the trade through on-the-job training.

Painters

Almost half of all painters are self-employed. They are among the last people needed to complete any construction job. They may need to show up on short notice. They may also need to work quickly, so tenants can move in fast. Painters may apply other finishes besides paint. These finishes include stains and varnishes. Training for painters is commonly done on the job.

CHAPTER 3
BLASTERS AND BUILDERS

Every construction project starts with a series of questions. What is the purpose of this project? Who will use it? Who will pay for it? Where will it be located? What will it look like? What impact will it have on the surrounding area?

Once these questions are answered, more questions need to be asked. Who will manage the project? Which materials will be used? When will the work start? When will it end? How many workers will be hired? What special skills will they need?

The answers to these questions — and many more — add up to a plan. This plan must be in place before any construction worker picks up a tool or puts on a hardhat.

Destruction and Construction

Let's suppose the planning has been done. The project is to build a skyscraper. The building has been designed. The money has been raised. The project managers are in place.

The first step is to prepare the site. If a building is already there, it will need to be removed. This is a job

Demolition workers imploded the Kingdome in March 2000 to make way for a new stadium in Seattle, Washington.

for **demolition** workers. Demolition crews may use a wrecking ball and other heavy equipment to knock down the building. Or they may use explosives to blow it up. Demolition workers will try to make the unwanted structure **implode**, or fall in on itself. They do this to avoid damaging buildings and hurting people in the surrounding area.

Laying the Groundwork

When the demolition workers have done their job, excavators clear the land. These and other heavy machines remove big rocks, shrubs, and tree stumps. Then the machines dig a large hole in the ground.

The soil must be carefully prepared so that it is firm enough to hold the weight of the building. The soil must also allow water to drain away from the site, so the lower floors do not flood. The excavation must be deep enough to fit all the underground floors.

Burj Dubai

World's Tallest Skyscrapers

The Burj Dubai is on its way to being the world's tallest skyscraper. This tower is located in the United Arab Emirates in the Middle East. The final height of the tower is being kept secret, but estimates have it reaching 2,684 feet (818 meters) tall. See how it stacks up against some other tall buildings:

- **Taipei 101**
  Location: Taipei, Taiwan
  Completed: 2004
  Height: 1,670 feet (509 m)

- **Shanghai World Financial Center**
  Location: Shanghai, China
  Completed: 2008
  Height: 1,614 feet (492 m)

- **Petronas Towers 1 & 2**
  Location: Kuala Lumpur, Malaysia
  Completed: 1998
  Height: 1,483 feet (452 m)

- **Sears Tower**
  Location: Chicago, Illinois
  Completed: 1974
  Height: 1,451 feet (442 m)

Sources: Council on Tall Buildings and Urban Habitats; Burj Dubai

A Firm Foundation

When the excavation work is finished, different construction crews work on the **foundation**. Many skyscrapers stand on concrete and metal **piles**. These piles are like very long, strong legs. The piles may extend downward hundreds of feet, all the way to the bedrock beneath the soil.

While workers pour the concrete and drive the piles for the foundation, other crews may also be at the site. These crews lay the pipes and cables that supply the building with basic services. Every office building needs water lines coming in and sewer lines going out. Electricians connect the building with the city's power grid and provide the building with telephone and Internet connections. Fire protection systems also must be installed.

Workers pour a load of concrete into a shallow foundation.

CHAPTER 4

OUTSIDE AND INSIDE JOBS

Some people like to work outside. They don't mind carrying heavy loads in the hot sun. They are willing to work long hours in cold weather. If you're one of those people, many construction jobs are right for you.

Highway construction workers are always exposed to weather. So are roofers. In the early stages of a building project, most construction jobs are outside jobs. Most inside jobs come later — after the **exterior** walls are built, floors are in place, and a roof is overhead.

Steel Beams and Scaffolding

As a skyscraper rises, you can see its steel and concrete skeleton growing higher and higher. Steel is a blend of iron and other materials. It is very hard, strong, and long-lasting. Steel bars and steel mesh can also be used to make concrete stronger. Steel bars used to reinforce concrete are called **rebars**.

The people who put together a building's skeleton are iron and metal workers. Teams of metal workers use cranes to raise heavy steel beams into position. Then other metal workers use special tools to attach the new beams to ones already there.

As a skyscraper rises in Seattle, Washington, iron and metal workers make sure beams and floors are correctly positioned.

Metal workers do difficult and dangerous work. On a skyscraper they work on scaffolding high above the ground. They use harnesses, nets, and other devices to be safe.

Skeleton and Skin

A big building project may take years to complete. Different workers with specific skills may work on parts of the building at the same time. For example, while metal workers continue to grow the building's skeleton, other workers wall in the lower floors.

Safety First

Construction workers have dangerous jobs. Construction sites are often called "hardhat areas." In these areas, workers and managers wear hardhats to keep their heads safe from falling objects. Construction companies and labor unions take worker safety very seriously. So does the Occupational Safety and Health Administration, or OSHA. OSHA is the main U.S. government agency that deals with worker safety. OSHA makes rules to protect construction workers.

Exterior walls are like a building's skin. In a house, they are usually made of wood, brick, or stone. In an office building, they may be made of glass, stone, metal, or concrete — or all these materials combined. Each material may require its own team of skilled workers.

Floor by Floor

After the floors and outer walls are in place, new teams start on the interior work. Stairways and elevators are installed. Electricians wire each level. Plumbers put together water and waste lines. Sheet metal workers build ducts for heating, cooling, and **ventilation**.

Ducts installed by sheet metal workers supply clean, fresh air to people inside a building.

As these basic systems are set up, more workers arrive. A skyscraper has many hallways, offices, and other rooms. The rooms on each floor are separated by inside walls and **partitions**. Carpenters may be called in to cut wood to support interior walls and doors. Drywall installers then put in wallboards and ceilings.

All interior walls and ceilings must look straight and smooth. Workers use lasers and other high-tech tools to make sure all parts fit well together.

Going Global

Construction is not only a way to make a good living. It's also a great way to see the world. Some large construction companies have offices around the globe.

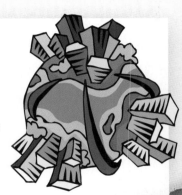

CHAPTER 5

FINISHING TOUCHES

Look around the room you're in right now. On the ceiling you might see paint, tiles, or plaster. On the windows? Drapes, shades, or blinds. On the walls? Paint or wallpaper. Beneath your feet? Wood, carpet, or vinyl flooring. The room may also hold built-in light fixtures, light switches, and electrical outlets. Some homeowners add these finishing touches. But in other kinds of construction, workers in the building trades do these jobs.

Completing the Interior

As a skyscraper reaches its final height, the structural work is almost done. But a tremendous amount of inside work is still unfinished. Some parts of the interior may be very fancy. Others, like basements and parking

A fresh coat of paint can make an older home look good — and a new home sparkle.

garages, will be quite plain. Many different workers need to apply their skills to the different areas.

Electricians make the final connections to wall sockets and switches. Plumbers make the final links to sinks and sprinklers. Plasterers work on the ceilings. Painters apply several coats of paint to the bare walls. Carpenters put in doorframes and doors. Glaziers work on glass windows, doors, and mirrors. Carpet installers lay down floor coverings. Tile setters apply tiles to bathroom walls and floors. All these jobs have a big role in creating a finished building.

Making a Home "Green"

"Green" homes save resources and reduce pollution. They also cut home heating and cooling bills. To meet homeowners' demands, construction workers need to know good ways to "go green." For example, plumbers may put in low-flow faucets and showers. They may also install toilets that use less

water. Builders may add solar panels (see image above) to generate electricity from the Sun.

Final Steps

As the inside work continues, workers on the outside are cleaning up the site. The scaffolding comes down. Giant cranes are taken apart and rolled away. Waste materials are hauled off and disposed of properly. These jobs are not glamorous, but they are important.

Meanwhile, other workers are readying the area around the new building. Concrete for sidewalks is poured. Parking lots are paved. The building entrance may be finished with beautiful wood, stone, glass, and works of art.

Finally, the day for the grand opening arrives. A few construction managers gaze proudly at the building they helped create. But by this time, nearly all the workers are busy with new projects.

Designed to save energy, the Hearst Tower is a "green" skyscraper in New York City.

CONSTRUCTION WORKER

OUTLOOK

- More than 9 million Americans have jobs in the building industry.
- The number of new jobs with construction firms is expected to grow by at least 10 percent between 2006 and 2016. In addition, many older workers are retiring and new ones will be needed.

WHAT YOU'LL DO

- Construction workers help build or repair houses, schools, hospitals, highways, skyscrapers, stadiums, and many other types of places.
- People in this field also help rebuild areas after disasters, such as Hurricane Katrina.
- Construction work involves many different skills. Some workers operate heavy earth-moving equipment, lay pipes, handle steel beams, or build brick or concrete walls. Others are roofers, electricians, plumbers, painters, or window installers — even demolition experts.
- You may work outdoors or indoors, depending on your specialty.

WHAT YOU'LL NEED

- Most jobs do not require a college degree. Many workers get on-the-job training. Others learn through apprentice programs.
- You'll need to be healthy and — for some tasks — physically tough. Many construction jobs are physically demanding.

WHAT YOU'LL EARN

- Many construction jobs pay more than $20 an hour, or more than $800 a week. Many workers earn overtime pay, too.

Source: U.S. Department of Labor, Bureau of Labor Statistics

GLOSSARY

apprentice — a beginner who learns a trade by working alongside an experienced worker

cranes — large, tall machines used for moving heavy objects

demolition — the act of destroying something, usually by knocking it down or blowing it up

drywall — a material (sometimes called wallboard or Sheetrock) that is used for interior walls and ceilings

excavators — heavy machines that dig or remove soil from a site

exterior — outside

foundation — the lowest part of a building

implode — to collapse inward

interior — inside

labor unions — groups formed by workers to protect their rights and improve their pay and working conditions

lasers — devices that emit an intense beam of light

partitions — light interior walls

pile drivers — machines used to force long piles into stone or earth

piles — columns of wood, steel, or reinforced concrete used to support a building

rebars — steel bars used in reinforced concrete

remodeling — making major changes in an existing building

scaffolding — a temporary structure, made of wood or metal, used by workers when constructing, cleaning, or repairing a building

trade contractors — firms or workers with special skills

ventilation — a system for bringing in fresh air and removing stale air and odors

vocational — related to work

TO FIND OUT MORE

Books

Building. Eyewitness Books (series). Philip Wilkinson (DK Publishing, 2000)

Construction. Discovering Careers for Your Future (series). 2nd ed. (Ferguson Publishing, 2008)

Construction Worker. High Interest Books (series). Rachel O'Connor (Children's Press, 2004)

Cool Careers for Girls in Construction. Cool Careers for Girls (series). Ceel Pasternak and Linda Thornburg (Impact Publications, 2000)

Skyscrapers. Uncovering Technology (series). Chris Oxlade (Firefly Books, 2006)

Stadiums. Building Amazing Structures (series). Chris Oxlade (Heinemann, 2000)

Web Sites

archKIDecture — Architecture for Kids
www.archkidecture.org

Learn the basics of building, plus do-it-yourself building projects.

HowStuffWorks: Buildings and Structures
science.howstuffworks.com/buildings-structures-channel.htm

Discover the science behind the construction industry.

Make It Happen: Building Careers — Secondary Students
www.buildingcareers.org/secondary

Check out this guide to construction careers, offered by the Home Builders Institute.

INDEX

About the Author

Geoffrey M. Horn has written more than three dozen books for young people and adults, along with hundreds of articles for encyclopedias and other works. He lives in southwestern Virginia, in the foothills of the Blue Ridge Mountains, with his wife, their collie, and six cats. He dedicates this book to Anna and Donald Strong and their three daughters.